Hot Bodes

Hot Sexy Lingerie & Swimsuit Girls Models Pictures

By **PHOTO ART LOVER**

www.ingramcontent.com/pod-product-compliance
Lightning Source LLC
Chambersburg PA
CBHW050419180526
45159CB00005B/2338